So Also in Christ

Re-Viewing the Plan of Salvation

BY NEAL PUNT

Library of Congress Cataloging-in-Publication Data

Punt, Neal.
  So also in Christ : re-viewing the plan of salvation / by Neal Punt.
      p. cm.
Includes index.
  ISBN 0-945315-23-6 (pbk.)
  1. Salvation.   2. Universalism–Biblical teaching.   3. Calvinism.
4. Arminianism.   I. Title.
  BT751.3 .P86 2002
  234–dc21

                                    2002001659

ISBN 0-945315-23-6

02 03 04 05 /CHG/ 5 4 3 2 1

TABLE OF CONTENTS

Introduction

It has been said that words are like eyeglasses on our soul. Through words we see people. We view them as relatives, friends, homeless persons, Christians, neighbors, Asians, Muslims, pagans, competitors, Jews, strangers, enemies, unbelievers, criminals, intellectuals, Africans, fellow workers, Russians, foreigners, etc. The list is nearly endless. We instinctively realize that these "eyeglasses" have a major effect on our attitude toward and how we relate to people.

In addition to these narrowly defined categories the Bible speaks of a final division of mankind — those who will be saved and those who will be lost. Without realizing it, we tend to view the human race as those who will be lost unless we have reason to think differently about certain individuals. How should we view our fellow human beings? To answer this question we must ask ourselves which of the following two statements do we believe best reflects the teaching of the Scriptures:

> A. All persons will be finally lost except those who the Bible declares will be saved.

> B. All persons will be saved except those who the Bible declares will be finally lost.

Our sin-damaged vision needs biblical correction. "A" and "B" are each a prescription for the "eyeglasses" we choose to wear. One prescription or the other will affect the way we view others and greatly modify our attitude towards and how we relate to them. The question is, does the Bible indicate which is the correct prescription to use?

The late J. Robert Spangler, Editor of *Ministry Magazine*, said this about my earlier book: "I carefully read your book, *What's Good About the Good News?* I must confess it has done something for my heart and my attitude toward the whole human race." He was moved by the scriptural principles found in that book. These same principles form the basis of this book intended for individual or small group study. May those who participate in this study undergo a similar experience.

Neal Punt

Chapter 1
Looking Back

The apostles turned "the world upside down" with "good news of great joy" that was "for all the people." That good news was that God was in Christ "reconciling the world to himself" (2 Cor. 5:19). This appears to have continued for the first few centuries of the Christian era in a way that is lacking in our versions of the gospel today. Undoubtedly there are many reasons for this difference.

Among these reasons is the fact that the early church fathers had an inclusive view of God's plan of salvation. Many erroneously believe that Origen (185–254 AD) was convicted by the church of his day for teaching that all persons will be saved. However, Origen was judged to be a heretic for his views regarding the Trinity. The early church tolerated his "universalism" (all persons will be saved), objecting only to the fact that he taught that all the saved would be equally rewarded.

Athanasius (293–373 AD) was so highly regarded as a stalwart defender of biblical orthodoxy that many years after his death he was honored by having his name associated with the creed that now bears his name. Athanasius believed that Jesus Christ purchased salvation and granted it to everyone without any exception. To be finally lost one had to reject the salvation already given to them.

Some theological historians have said that if any view of salvation similar to the one we will consider in this study is found it will be among the early church fathers. Dr. Roger Olson, whose book *The Story of Christian Theology* won Christianity Today's 2000 Book Award, writes: "I do not know of any systematic theology prior to your own publications that spells out the nature of salvation as you do. But I hear distant echoes of it (foreshadowings, adumbrations) in Athanasius and perhaps other early church fathers" (Quoted with permission.).

Those who were closest (in time) to the apostles had an inclusive view of God's plan of salvation. For the most part they taught that all will be saved with no exceptions or that all will be saved with some exceptions. This may not seem so strange to us after we consider the so-called "universalistic" passages of the Bible in Chapter 3.

It was not until the later part of the fourth century that most theologians began to view the plan of salvation in the restrictive form with which we are familiar, that is, "All persons will be finally lost, except those the Bible tells us will be saved." Ever since that time mainstream Christian theologians have attempted to define the "exceptions," that is, those who will be saved. Such restrictive definitions of those who will be saved are not found among the leading church fathers in the first, second and third centuries.

Pelagius (about 350–418 AD), usually described as a pious British monk, was concerned that Christians were becoming lax in their lifestyle. For this reason he began to teach that everyone will be lost except those who, by their own strength and determination of will, would live in obedience to the law of God, following the example of Christ.

Augustine (354–430 AD) recognized in Pelagianism an unacceptable works-righteousness. He taught that all will be lost except those who God in his eternal, sovereign, incomprehensible grace has chosen to bring to salvation. A middle position between these two was that of the semi-Pelagianists. They proposed that all will be lost except those who, by their own sovereign decision, accept God's offer of salvation.

In the Middle Ages the accepted belief became: "All will be lost except those who live in continuing fellowship with the church." This belief deteriorated into a source of controlling power not only for the Roman church but also for the Roman Empire during Constantine's rule. Few were willing to risk their eternal destiny by challenging the Roman church's definition of those who would be saved.

The Reformers of the sixteenth century would have no more of this. They emphasized a need for a personal commitment of faith. "The just shall live by faith." In place of: "No salvation outside the Church" the motto became "No salvation outside the household of faith." Today Christians commonly hold that all persons will be lost except those who make and maintain a personal commitment of faith.

Following the Reformation there is little agreement on how any sinner can believe because "there is no one who does good, not even one" (Romans 1:18–3:20). From where does the ability to believe come? Among the many answers that have been proposed we find these; (A) there are traces of original goodness that remain in every sinner; (B) God has planted a seed of faith in every sinner's heart; (C) there is an enabling grace that attends the Word whenever it is preached; (D) from eternity God foresaw all those who would of their own accord believe; (E) by sovereign grace God creates faith in all those chosen to salvation; (F) various combinations of these views that account for the ability of those totally corrupted by sin to be able to believe.

"All the king's horses and all the king's men" have not been able to put these various views together again. Evangelical Christianity has not been able to come to a common definition of those who will be saved and how they become so.

What is at stake here is not the sort of technical question of doctrine important only for theologians. At issue is the eternal lot of mankind. The teachings of the Scriptures concerning the grace and judgment of God are not something we may leave to professional theologians. The message of salvation is at the very heart of the gospel, and what one believes about it will have broad implications and far-reaching consequences for every aspect of the Christian life.

Throughout this study it will be extremely important to keep the distinction between objective and subjective salvation in mind. This can not be emphasized too strongly. Many misunderstandings will develop if we forget this distinction.

We can see the importance of this distinction by considering that the apostle Paul said: "I have become all things to all men so that by all possible means I might save some" (1 Cor. 9:22). Did Paul ever "*save*" anyone? Of course not, Jesus is the *only* Savior! This irrefutable answer alerts us to the fact that the Bible makes a good and absolutely necessary distinction between "objective" and "subjective" salvation.

Objective salvation refers to the work accomplished by Christ nearly 2,000 years ago. By his perfect life and sacrificial death he objectively saved every human being who will be finally saved. Their salvation was made certain when he said, "It is finished." "By one sacrifice he has made perfect forever those who are being made holy" (Heb. 10:14). Our eternal security is based on this fact. The Bible speaks of objective salvation as "the gospel *of* your salvation" (Eph. 1:13).

In this study, the expressions "elect in Christ" and "those who will be saved" refer to those whose salvation has been objectively accomplished by their identity with Christ in his death and resurrection. They are those who will surely come to fullness of new life in Christ.

Subjective salvation occurs when the Holy Spirit transforms the sinner's heart, soul, and mind so that he or she desires to live in obedience to God's will. That is to say, their regeneration, their new birth, their conversion may occur at any point in time during their earthly life. The Bible refers to this as the gospel "*for*" salvation (Rom. 1:13).

It is only in this subjective sense that Paul or anyone else can be an instrument used by God to *subjectively* save those who are already *objectively* saved by Jesus Christ.

Paul was objectively saved before he set out for Damascus. He was chosen "in Him *before the creation of the world*" (Eph. 1:4). Therefore Paul speaks of "this grace that was given us in Christ Jesus *before the beginning of time*" (2 Tim. 1:9). Paul was set "apart from birth" (Gal. 1:15). Was Paul a Christian or converted before he started toward Damascus? Clearly not! Thus, a person can be objectively saved and yet be neither a Christian nor converted.

Discussion Questions:

1. Many ways have been proposed to account for the fact that sinners, totally corrupted by sin, are enabled to believe. Which one do you think is correct?

2. For more than 1,600 years those who have looked to the Bible are still widely divided on the question, "How are those totally corrupted by sin enabled to believe?" What do you think accounts for this lack of consensus?

3. When it is reported that, as a result of an evangelism effort, a number of persons were "saved," is this a reference to objective or subjective salvation? Do the following verses refer to objective or subjective salvation? Acts 2:41; Acts 2:47; 2 Cor. 5:19; Heb. 10:14; Acts 16:14b; 1 John 2:2; John 3:16; John 3:17; John 3:18.

4. Can only those who are objectively saved be subjectively saved?

5. It has been said that objective salvation can be likened to the Emancipation Proclamation. When President Lincoln signed that proclamation every slave in the confederate states was objectively a free person; however, no slave was subjectively free and able to enjoy that freedom until they heard about and believed the proclamation. What do you think of this analogy?

Chapter 2
It Makes a Difference

The silhouette of the goblet on the cover of this book demonstrates that our mind interprets what we see. A person who has never seen a goblet would recognize only the faces. Whether we see the faces or the goblet depends on past experience. By concentrating we can direct our mind to see either the faces or the goblet.

Something similar happens when we read the Bible. If we accept the fact that some persons will not be saved, there are two ways of viewing the overall message of God's Word. Either (1) all persons will be lost except those the Bible tells us will be saved; or, (2) all persons will be saved except those the Bible tells us will be lost. In the Introduction we referred to these as prescriptions "A" and "B" for the eyeglasses through which we see the world of humanity.

The Bible speaks of two men, two "Adams"—one at the dawn of history, the other "in the fullness of time." Through the disobedience of the first Adam condemnation and death came into this world. The obedience of the second Adam (Jesus Christ) brought salvation and life.

We can so concentrate our attention on the first Adam that we envision all mankind involved in his disobedience having brought corruption, condemnation, and death on themselves. Entering this dark picture are separate circles of light shining upon those who by God's grace will be saved. The other possibility is that we give the crucified and risen Savior the place of preeminence and through him we see the world (of people) bathed in the light of his glorious grace. Some persons do not enjoy this light for no other reason than that they love darkness rather than the light (John 3:19).

There are some for whom the first picture of a fallen mankind due to Adam's sin has been so deeply etched on their mind that they find it impossible to see the second picture. And there are others who see the two ways of viewing the Bible's message and are not impressed. It does not change either the number of person who will be saved or the way in which God saves them. Nothing actually changes, so why bother about it?

But there are still others who begin to see the gracious work that was accomplished by Christ for the children of men. This new insight has a dramatic effect upon their life. They begin to see God, themselves, and others in a new way and it brings to them a joy, a peace, and a delight in God's plan of salvation they had not known before.

The two views are not merely a play on words; they make a real difference. True reformation never begins in the world "out there." The difference in how we view mankind will be a change within our heart and mind. Our perceptions form our attitudes. Our attitudes, in turn, affect the way we relate to God, to ourselves, and to all other human beings wherever and in whatever circumstances we meet them. Christians ought to view themselves as children of God and to view all other human beings in the same way.

Imagine for a moment viewing and affirming yourself and everyone you meet as an elect child of God for whom Christ died. What a reformation would take place in your life! Wouldn't you find it much easier to love your enemies and to pray for those who despitefully use you?"

Is there a biblical basis for respecting ourselves as children of God and for treating all other human beings with the same respect?

We cannot say that we will not adopt one view or the other. In spite of all denials, it is impossible to read, interpret, or bring the gospel to others without working with one assumption or the other.

Ever since the time of Augustine (Chapter 1) most Bible scholars have assumed that all persons will be lost except those of whom it is expressly revealed that they will be saved. This assumption is so basic, so commonly held, and so pervasive in Christian theology and tradition that we feel uncomfortable calling it into question.

It must be noted, however, that this prevailing assumption has distorted the universal accents of the Scriptures so that they are not accepted as an essential and joyous characteristic of the "Good News." This unexamined assumption has deprived many sincere Christians of the assurance of their salvation and has often placed believers in doubt as to whether they should press the claims of Christ's kingship upon everyone everywhere. It has detracted from the positive, world-embracing, thrilling good news of what God in Christ has done for mankind. Consequently God is not praised as fully and joyfully as he desires to be.

Dr. Charles Hodge, the Princeton Calvinist, worked with the traditional assumption in nearly all of his writings. On one occasion he caught a glimpse of the other way of viewing God's work in Christ. He expressed it as follows:

> "All the descendants of Adam, except Christ, are under condemnation; all the descendants of Adam, except those of whom it is expressly revealed that they cannot inherit the kingdom of God, are saved" (*Systematic Theology*, 1888, Vol. I, P. 26).

Here Hodge claims that all who are condemned in Adam are saved in Christ "except those of whom it is expressly revealed that they cannot inherit the kingdom of God." Two paragraphs later Hodge asserts that this perspective is grounded on the very nature of God because, "It is more congenial with the nature of God to bless than to curse, to save than to destroy."

Hodge claims that Romans 5:18 teaches that the work of Christ has counteracted that of Adam in every instance *except* of those individuals of whom it is expressly revealed in Scripture that they will not share in the benefits of Christ's redemption. Note carefully that Hodge does not say that all persons were united with Christ in his death and resurrection but subsequently some of them were removed from this union. That was Athanasius's view (Chapter 1). Such a view would contradict the scriptural teaching of the eternal security of those who are "in Christ" as well as John 3:36, which teaches that the wrath of God "rests upon" those who disobey the Son—that is to say, God's wrath remains on them, having never been removed.

Eternal salvation is not the kind of gift that can be returned or rejected by the person who has received it. If it were returnable it would not be eternal salvation. Redemption is Christ's gracious work whereby he sets his people free from their sin and rescues them from eternal death. Redemption has not occurred for those who pay the penalty of sin and enter eternal death. Those who will finally be lost were never "elect in Christ," they were never given the gift of salvation.

In this study we find that we have biblical warrant for viewing all persons as children of God, those for whom Christ died, until and unless we have knowledge to the contrary. By "biblical warrant" we mean that the Bible permits, authorizes, and even requires us to view all persons as children of God. That is, we are to love, respect, and relate to each of them as if he or she is a person for whom Christ died.

This biblical warrant is not a judgment about the nature of the person addressed. The person may, in fact, not be one of God's elect—a person for whom Christ died. This warrant indicates the approach we should take in leading them to the Lord. Paul says, "So from now on we regard no one from a worldly point of view" (2 Cor. 5:16–21). We have the right and the duty to assume they are children of God, a new creation, unless and until we have knowledge to the contrary.

We will not have such knowledge to the contrary concerning any particular person or group of persons until the Last Day, no matter how evil they appear to be. Early in his life the apostle Paul certainly appeared to be outside of Christ even though he belonged to Christ from the day of his birth (Gal. 1:13–15). Consider this worst-case scenario: A person confronted by Jesus himself rejects Jesus and the words he speaks. Wouldn't we at that very moment judge that he or she is among those who will be lost? However, such a negative judgement can not be made about anyone until "the last day" (John 12:47, 48).

Imagine for a moment that everyone in a congregation would view and affirm themselves and everyone they meet as children of God for whom Christ died. What a glorious light would radiate from that church! No one would be looked upon as an outsider. Feeding the hungry, giving something to drink to the thirsty, inviting strangers in, and visiting the sick and those in prison would be rewarded as having been done to one of the "brothers" of Jesus (Matt. 25:40).

It may be helpful to think of the premise we develop in this study as *qualified* Universalism. The necessary limiting qualification to Universalism (all will be saved) is so clearly revealed in the Scriptures (See Chapter 4) that we need not hesitate to call this teaching Biblical Universalism (See p. 83).

Discussion Questions:

1. When a pastor addresses the congregation as "Beloved in the Lord" does he do so because he has certain knowledge that everyone there is an elect child of God? If not, what is the significance of this greeting? Should he do so if there is a possibility that some are not elect in Christ?

2. When a person is convinced that he or she is among those who will be saved does this have any practical effect in their everyday life? In what ways?

3. Would treating all persons as children of God mean that there is no place for punishment in human relationships? Why or why not? (Heb. 12:9)

4. How would most people respond if you asked them whether "A" or "B," as stated in the Introduction, reflects the Bible's teaching?

5. Does the word "brothers" in Matthew 25:40 mean that only those things done (vv. 37–39) for believers will be rewarded? If the answer is yes, what does the term "stranger" mean in verse 38? In what ways does Biblical Universalism help us understand the word "brothers" in Matthew 25:40?

Chapter 3
All - Every - The World

Some of the most familiar and best-loved verses in the New Testament say that *all* persons will find salvation in Christ. John the Baptist introduces Jesus, "Look, the Lamb of God, who takes away the sin of *the world*!" (John 1:29). About his death Jesus says, "And I, when I am lifted up from the earth, will draw *all men* to myself" (John 12:32). Paul explains the benefits of Christ's resurrection: "For as in Adam *all* die, so also in Christ *all* will be made alive" (1 Cor. 15:22).

The title of this book, **"So Also In Christ,"** is taken from 1 Cor. 15:22. This and other so-called "universalistic" texts pose a dilemma for Bible-believing Christians. Although these passages appear to teach that *all persons* will be saved, elsewhere the Bible plainly reveals that not everyone will be saved (Chapter 4). We may not resolve this apparent contradiction by simply closing our eyes to what the following so-called "universalistic" texts clearly say:

John 1:9 "The true light that gives light to *every* man was coming into the world."

John 1:29 "Look, the Lamb of God, who takes away the sin of *the world*!"

John 3:17 "For God did not send his Son into the world

to condemn the world, but to save *the world* through him."

John 12:32 "But I, when I am lifted up from the earth, will draw *all* men to myself."

John 12:47 "For I did not come to judge *the world*, but to save it."

Romans 5:18 "Consequently, just as the result of one trespass was condemnation for *all* men, so also the result of one act of righteousness was justification that brings life for *all* men."

Romans 11:32 "For God has bound *all* men over to disobedience so that he may have mercy on them *all.*"

1 Corinthians 15:22 "For as in Adam *all* die, so also in Christ *all* will be made alive."

2 Corinthians 5:14 "For Christ's love compels us, because we are convinced that one died for *all*, and therefore *all* died."

2 Corinthians 5:19 "God was reconciling *the world* to himself in Christ, not counting men's sins against them."

Philippians 2:10, 11 "That at the name of Jesus *every* knee should bow, ...and *every* tongue confess that Jesus Christ is Lord."

Colossians 1:20 "Through him to reconcile to himself *all* things, whether things on earth or things in heaven, by making peace through his blood, shed on the cross."

1 Timothy 2:6 "Who gave himself a ransom for *all* men."

1 Timothy 4:10 "Who is the Savior of *all* men, especially of those who believe."

Titus 2:11 (RSV) "For the grace of God has appeared for the salvation of *all* men."

Hebrews 2:9 "He suffered death, so that by the grace of God he might taste death for *everyone*."

1 John 2:2 "He is the atoning sacrifice for our sins, and not only for ours but also for the sins of *the whole world*."

Ever since the middle of the fourth century the conventional thinking has been that to accept these passages as written would necessarily mean that all persons, without exception, will be saved. Such Absolute Universalism contradicts the teaching of God's Word, namely, some persons will be finally lost.

After the Reformation this dilemma has been dealt with by two schools of thought associated with the names of James Arminius and John Calvin. Arminians resolve the problem by denying that these passages speak of an actual, certain-to-be-realized salvation. Calvinists take the other road and deny that these texts have reference to all persons.

Although we have considered most of the arguments presented by both of these theological traditions we need not and cannot do so in this brief study. What we can do is illustrate that neither tradition has accepted these passages as written.

Calvinists correctly recognize that these passages, within their immediate context, plainly speak of an actual, certain-to-be-realized salvation. That is, they refer to all elect persons. "Jesus saves," they say, "he doesn't just make salvation possible." Because the Bible elsewhere reveals that some persons will not be saved, Calvinists insist that these verses can not refer to "all persons" distributively (head for head).

To make their view appear plausible, Calvinists claim that in some of these passages the terms "all" or "all men" refer merely to "both Jews and Gentiles." This overlooks the fact that the Bible has no difficulty in making reference to "both Jews and Gentiles" when it wishes to do so (See Acts 14:5; 19:10; 20:21; Rom., 3:9; 1 Cor. 1:24).

Sometimes the words "all" and "every" and the phrase "all men," Calvinists argue, mean "all classes of men." In Titus 2:11 this claim is supposedly strengthened by the fact that various classes of persons are mentioned in the preceding ten verses. A closer look reveals that Paul's logic runs in the opposite direction. It is because "the grace of God has appeared for the salvation of all men" (Titus 2:11 RSV) that various classes of persons are mentioned in the preceding verses, as the word "For" at the beginning of verse 11, indicates.

Furthermore, "classes of people" is an abstraction that exists only in one's mind. This abstraction neither needs nor is capable of receiving "salvation." To bring this abstraction back into reality it is said that these verses really mean "some people of all classes." This is so far removed from what these verses actually say that this explanation has to be rejected out of hand. There is no language in which it is possible to refer to "some persons of all classes" by the single words "all" or "every" or the phrase "all men."

Arminians correctly contend that these passages, within their immediate context, clearly refer to all men, that is, they refer to every human being without exception. "Whatever Christ has done for one sinner," they say, "he has done for every sinner." In light of the fact that some persons will not be saved, Arminians insist that these verses can not have reference to an actual, certain-to-be-realized salvation.

Arminians, therefore, simply and quite arbitrarily insist that these passages must be speaking of merely a potential or possible salvation or of God's willingness to save all persons. But there is nothing in the immediate context that even hints that these verses intend only a potential or possible salvation.

Calvinists discard the "all men" aspect of these texts and Arminians close their eyes to the "will be saved" element of these passages. Without realizing it, both of these schools of thought have permitted their theology to determine what these texts may say. Yet both sides agree that the Scriptures, as written, ought to shape their theology!

For every ten Calvinistic scholars who show beyond all reasonable doubt that these texts speak of "an actual, certain-to-be- realized" salvation, there are another ten Arminian theologians of equal credibility who just as convincingly demonstrate that these texts most assuredly relate to "every person." This futile debate has been carried on for more than 400 years.

One is tempted to say, "Forget these differences, let's just work together to save souls." Any such indifference toward what the Word of God actually says in these passages is a far cry from the commendable attitude of the early church: "They received the message with great eagerness and examined the Scriptures every day to see if what Paul said was true" (Acts 17:11). How we understand the so-called "universalistic" texts will have a major impact on our motivation for and the message we ought to bring in outreach ministries (Chapters 8 and 9).

In ordinary conversation we often use the words "all," "every," and "world" with limitations that are clearly understood from the immediate context. Occasionally we also find such usage in the Bible. This causes no confusion. However, there are no limitations in the immediate context of these so-called "universalistic" passages. These passages are not unclear or fuzzy. We have no right to limit the scope of their reference, other than the limitation that is imposed on them by the teaching of the Scriptures in their broader context (Chapter 5).

There are truly learned, evangelical, Calvinist professors contending that these passages speak so clearly of a certain-to-be-realized salvation that they cannot possibly have reference to "all men." A few miles down the road, equally learned, Bible-believing professors in the Arminian tradition are teaching the next generation that so clearly do these same passages speak in terms of all persons they cannot possibly be speaking of a "certain-to-be-realized" salvation.

The result is that the Absolute Universalists (everyone will be saved) have walked off with the prize. They alone have accepted these passages as written. This sad spectacle is repeated every day in many different places. Either we accept these passages as written without any exceptions (Absolute Universalism) or we accept them as written with the exceptions that are necessarily imposed on them by the broader context of the Scriptures as a whole (Biblical Universalism). No one has been able to suggest a third way of accepting these passages as written.

We need not be Greek scholars to be able to discern what these passages say. They read in Greek just as they do in our accepted English translations. Translators have not had the same problem with these so-called "universalistic" texts as theologians have had. The 400-year-old Arminian/Calvinist debate has demonstrated with finality that the translators have given us an accurate translation of these texts.

Bernard Baruch has correctly observed, "Every man has a right to his opinion, but no man has a right to be wrong in his facts." The fact is: **The so-called "universalistic" texts speak of a certain-to-be-realized salvation as Calvinists have consistently maintained and they do so in terms of all persons as Arminians have always affirmed.** (See "1", p. 83)

Discussion Questions:

1. It has been said that "all will be made alive" in 1 Cor. 15:22 refers to the "physical resurrection" of *all* persons at the end of the age. Will *all* persons be physically raised from death? (See 1 Thess. 4:17) Does the first part of this verse refer merely to "physical death"? Does this resurrection have anything to do with the forgiveness of sins? (See v. 17) Does the Bible ever use the phrase "in Christ" to designate a person who will be finally lost? (See 2 Cor. 5:17)

2. In Greek as well as in English the word order of 1 Cor. 15:22 is "in Christ all" not "all in Christ." What would be the difference?

3. Would it be better to discard the "all men" aspect of the so-called "universalistic" texts or the "will be saved" element? May we disregard either one or the other?

4. What conclusion do you draw from the fact that theologians, not Bible translators, have a problem with the so-called "universalistic" texts?

Chapter 4
Who Will Be Finally Lost?

The title of this chapter is based on the assumption that some persons will be finally lost. Before answering the question we must say something about that assumption.

Throughout the history of the church there has been a minority who denies that some persons will be finally lost. They believe that every person, without exception, will find salvation in Christ either in this life or in a future existence. This belief system is called Universalism, Absolute Universalism, or Restoration Theology. As strange as it may seem, evangelical Christians in increasing numbers are accepting this view. "It is a consummation devoutly to be wished," as Shakespeare might say. But wishing does not make it so.

Universalism is among the most appealing and destructive errors seeping into the church today. It is the original lie of Satan tailored for a humanity already in sin. Its message to everyone is, "Even though you may endure the purging of God's judgment, *you will not die.*" It is more deceptive than its brief original form because it is presented as the result of the work accomplished by Christ.

Universalists find their strongest argument in the so-called "universalistic" texts. This is understandably so.

These passages speak of actual salvation in terms of all persons as we noted in Chapter 3. Our zeal to refute Universalism does not give us permission to distort or deny what those passages clearly say. We will look for a resolution of this problem in the next chapter.

Few truths are more obvious to those who read this book than that there will be a final division of mankind, the saved and those who will be finally lost. An extensive refutation of Universalism would be preaching to the choir. We need not even consider the explicit testimony of Scripture as found in such passages as 2 Thess. 1:9, "They will be punished with everlasting destruction and shut out from the presence of the Lord and from the majesty of his power on the day he comes" (See also Matt. 7:23; 25:41,46; John 5:28, 29; 2 Thess. 2:12; etc.). Let us bring attention to two subtle arguments that are used by Universalists.

Parents never abandon their children except that those parents are either sinful or weak. God, the Holy Father, with unlimited ability and resources will never finally forsake any of his children. Even though a mother may "have no compassion on the child she has born," (Isa. 49:15), God will not forget any of his children. It necessarily follows, "If we are children, then we are heirs...co-heirs with Christ" (Rom. 8:17). Therefore, the Universalists say, no one will be finally lost.

If the assumption underneath this argument is valid, the argument is irrefutable. The assumption is that all human beings are children of God by virtue of their creation in the image of God. This popular theme is seldom challenged. Although Adam and Eve were created in the image of God, they were not created as God's children. The Scriptures know of only two ways to be part of God's family: through natural generation (Christ alone is the eternal, natural Son of God) and by adoption (we are adopted children of God). Even sinless human beings would require adoption into God's family.

Biological ancestry does not make one a member of God's family! "Do not think you can say to yourselves, 'We have Abraham as our father.' I tell you that out of these stones God can raise up children for Abraham" (Matt. 3:9). The stuff we are made of, whether common ancestry or stones, does not make us or prevent us from becoming children of Abraham with God as our Father. "If you belong to Christ, then you are Abraham's seed" (Gal. 3:29).

Another subtle argument used by Universalists is this: Every person will be saved because everyone created in God's image is of infinite value. Again, this is an irrefutable argument if the premise is valid. God is neither so foolish nor so weak as to be deprived of something that has infinite value.

So much good would result if all human beings were treated as though they had infinite value that we like to think this hyperbole is literally true. But nothing created can be of infinite value. If it were, the essential distinction between the Creator and what is created would be breached.

Furthermore, to say that every sinner will be saved because he or she has infinite value does an injustice to the gracious character of God's saving act. Each sinner is not a "hidden treasure," or a "pearl of great price" sought after by God because they have inherent value. Such a teaching contradicts the scriptural truth that he saved us "because of his own purpose and grace [undeserved favor]" (2 Tim. 1:9). The fact that we are mere creatures saved by grace, not on the basis of worth, requires us to recognize that human beings are not of infinite value.

Some Universalists speak of a "greater hope." The reference is to the hope that God's punishments in the here-after are meant to lead to salvation. It is true that all must appear before the judgment seat of Christ. Each will receive what is due him or her, for the things done in the body, whether good or bad (2 Cor. 5:10). This can be neither a punishment nor a form of purification for the sins of those who are in Christ Jesus. This is the judgment scene where-in "those on his right" are publicly awarded for the good they have done and the "those on his left" are publicly judged for the evil they have done (Compare Matt. 25:35, 36 with Matt. 25:42, 43.).

Those who desire such a "greater hope" can do so only at the cost of giving up the far, far "greater hope" expressed in these familiar words: "Jesus paid it all, all to him I owe." Jesus is the sin-bearer who bore all the sins of all his people. The biblical evidence for this truth is so extensive that we can cite only a fraction of it here: "The Lord has laid on him the iniquity of us all" (Isa. 53:6); "It is finished" (John 19:30); "The blood of Jesus, his Son, purifies us from all sin" (1 John 1:7).

The suggested "greater hope" denigrates the perfect work Christ accomplished for his own in that he *has removed* all our sins from us as far as east is from the west. Why is it necessary for those whose sin was removed by Christ's blood to continue to experience the consequence of their sin after their life upon earth? Is there something that sinners must do or an attitude they must display before God can or will translate them to glory? If so, then the teaching of Scripture concerning salvation by sovereign grace is compromised.

We now turn to the question, "Who will be finally lost?"

It is very important to notice that the question is not, "Who deserves to be finally lost?" The answer to this question is crystal-clear: "all men." Due to the fall and disobedience of our first parents, all persons except Jesus Christ are conceived and born in sin. Consequently, every one of them deserves eternal death and God has placed them under the sentence of death. "The result of one trespass was condemnation for all men" (Rom. 5:18a).

Romans 1:18–3:20 and parallel passages reveal the corruption and blameworthiness of all persons that result from their sin in Adam (original sin). These passages give us a picture of every person who is not born again and every child of God before he or she was born again. They reveal the fact that "All have turned away, they have together become worthless; there is no one who does good, not even one" (Rom. 3:12). The teaching of original sin does not distinguish those who will be saved from those who will be finally lost. The doctrine of original sin does not tell us whether many or few, all or none, will be finally lost.

Who will be finally lost? As a consequence of Adam's sin all his descendants, except Jesus Christ, were born sinful by nature and justly sentenced to eternal death. However, nowhere in all of Scripture do we read—nor is it implied, nor is it to be inferred—that anyone ever suffers eternal death by reason of their sin in Adam, *apart from* individual, willful, final unbelief and sin on the part of the person so rejected.

In 1977 an official complaint was registered against the Reformed creeds charging that these creeds teach that some persons are consigned to hell solely on the basis of original sin, thus allowing the possibility that some persons are consigned to hell before they are born. A committee was appointed to study this complaint that has often been alleged against Calvinism. After three years of study the committee's report (Study Report 30) was adopted by the 1980 Synod of the Christian Reformed Church and was confirmed by the 1981 Synod.

This report was sent to all the churches of the CRC to shed light on the biblical and creedal teaching regarding those who will be finally lost (the Reprobate). All page references are to the 1980 Acts of Synod:

According to Report 30, the basis or cause of condemnation (consignment to hell, eternal death) is: man's "sin" (pp. 516, 517); "sin and unbelief" (seven times, pp. 516, 517, 522, 548 [twice], 553, and 554). "God consigns to destruction only on the basis of what that person does and whatever evil actions that person performs" (p. 521). "So can we say that God rejects only those who reject him? Most emphatically we can" (p. 521). "Damnation is a response to the evil the 'reprobates' do" (p. 522). "They themselves are the agents of unbelief" (p. 530). An agent is one who acts for himself or for another person.

This official elucidation continues—"God condemns to destruction only those who do, in fact, sin and exhibit unbelief" (p. 530). "Human beings are condemned only on the basis of what they actually do in history" (p. 530). "Those not selected have disqualified themselves through their sins" (p. 537). "The condition of the nonelect results from their unbelief" (p. 538). "Condemnation, however, is to be found solely in the persistent unbelief and sin of those so condemned" (p. 553).

For 17 years before this report appeared I had searched, and asked others to search, the Scriptures to determine who will be finally lost. I had come to the same conclusion (See *Unconditional Good News*, Eerdmans, 1980) as Report 30—that no one will be finally lost *apart from* individual, willful, persistent sin on the part one consigned to eternal death. Therefore it is a good and necessary implication of both Report 30 and Biblical Universalism that all who die in infancy are saved.

All who are finally lost will be lost for one reason only. That is because they persistently, knowingly, and willfully rejected or remained indifferent to God's truth, kindness, and company, however it was revealed to them during their lives on earth (John 3:19). They will have consciously said no to God and insisted on living apart from him.

The biblical teaching is that—**All persons, except Jesus Christ, are liable for and polluted by the imputed sin of Adam (original sin). However, the Scriptures do not teach or imply that anyone is consigned to eternal damnation solely on the basis of their sin in Adam *apart from* actual, willful and persistent sin on the part of the person so consigned.** (See p. 83)

Discussion Questions:

1. All persons are members of the "human family." Does this mean that all are God's children?

2. Are human beings of "greater value" than other animals?

3. How does the teaching of a "greater hope" differ from the Roman Catholic teaching of purgatory? Might you hear a "hell fire" sermon in a Universalist Church?

4. What does the teaching of original sin *not* do?

5. Does Report 30 teach that judgment against original sin has been removed for everyone? What does the conclusion reached by Report 30 necessarily say about all those who die in infancy?

Chapter 5
All Are... Some Are Not

It certainly looks like we have painted ourselves into a corner. Chapter 3 concludes with the fact that the so-called "universalistic" texts speak of a certain-to-be-realized salvation in terms of all persons. Chapter 4 recognizes that some persons will not be saved. The title of this chapter purposefully reflects this apparent dilemma.

An internationally known theologian said he knew why the view presented in this study has not been broadly accepted. He explained, "This reticence is due to the fact that what you are proposing is not coherent. The two biblical facts are contradictory. If the first [Chapter 3] is true, all must be saved. But according to the second [Chapter 4] they are not. It is repugnant to believe contraries."

This apparent contradiction does not arise out the premise of Biblical Universalism (See p. 83). It arises from the fact that every branch of Christian theology has failed to recognize the distinction that must be made between universal statements and generalizations. These are often confused, but there is a world of difference between them.

Universals, by definition, allow no exceptions. Generalizations are universal declarations that have known exceptions. Generalizations are often used in the Bible as well as in other literature. They are far more common than universals. Failure to recognize that the so-called "universalistic" texts (Chapter 3) are generalizations, *not* universals, has caused major divisions within the Christian church.

Because they insist that these passages are universals, Calvinists contend that they must refer to all persons elect in Christ *without exception.* For the same reason, Arminians claim that these passages undoubtedly speak of a potential salvation for all persons *without exception.* Universalists make the same error and conclude that these texts proclaim actual salvation for all persons *without exception.*

These three schools of thought recognize that the universal declarations "all have sinned" as found in 1 Kings 8:46; Ps. 14:3; Eccles. 7:20; Romans 3:9, 10, 12, 23: Romans 5:12, 18a; 1 John 1:8,10 etc. have an exception. There is no exception in the immediate contexts. The broader context of Scripture, however, provides an exception: "The corruption spread, by God's just judgment, from Adam to all his descendants—*except for Christ alone.*" We must keep in mind that "Jesus Christ" is an exception to the many universal declarations that "all have sinned."

Whatever the Bible says it says from within its entire context. When the so-called "universalistic" texts speak of an accomplished, actual, certain-to-be-realized salvation in terms of all persons, they may *never* be understood apart from the exceptions that are found in the broader context of Scripture of which they are a part. These texts (Chapter 3) are like fish out of water, having no sustainable life of their own when they are read in isolation from the rest of the Bible.

The Bible alerts us to the fact that its universal declarations may have exceptions not found in the immediate context of the declaration. "For he 'has put everything under his feet'" (1 Cor. 15:27a). This universal declaration is taken from Psalm 8:6. It is also found in Hebrews 2:8 with this qualifying phrase added: "In putting everything under him, God left nothing that is not subject to him." There is not a hint of any exception in the immediate context of either of these references.

However, this clear-cut, emphatic universal declaration has an exception. First Cor. 15:27b continues, "Now when it [the Bible] says that 'everything' has been put under him, it is clear that this does not include God himself, who put everything under Christ." 1 Cor. 15:27 tells us that when we read Psalm 8:6 and Hebrews 2:8 we must supply the exception found in the broader context of the Bible.

We can draw this parallel to 1 Cor. 15:27: "Now when the Bible says that 'all persons will be saved in Christ' [in the so-called "universalistic" texts, (Chapter 3)], it is clear that this does not include those who the Bible says will not be saved."

When reading the Scriptures we are frequently required to supply the exceptions to its universal declarations. Many passages declare that "All men sinned." Nevertheless there was one who "knew no sin." "He has put everything under his feet. In putting everything under him, God left nothing that is not subject to him" (Ps. 8:6, Heb. 2:8). However, "this does not include God himself" (1 Cor. 15:27). "Everything is permissible for me," says Paul (1 Cor. 6:12). Everything? "With God all things are possible" (Matt. 19:26); yet God "cannot disown himself" (2 Tim. 2:13).

Prayers should be made "for all men" (1 Tim. 2:1); but not for the dead and possibly not for some others (1 John 5:16). "Everyone in the province...deserted me" (2 Tim. 1:15). The following verse speaks of an exception, etc.

As long as we are mindful of the exceptions we can accept these universal declarations as written: All men sinned. God did put all things under Christ's feet. All things were permissible for Paul. With God all things are possible. We ought to pray for all persons. All did turn away from Paul. The exceptions do not negate, they merely limit, the basic truth set forth in the universal declaration.

We make a serious error either if we do not accept the truth proclaimed in the Bible's universal declarations or if we overlook the exceptions that must be understood from the broader context of the Bible. For example, some persons claim that we can say nothing about the eternal destiny of those who die without having heard the gospel, because the Bible tells us nothing about this question. That is God's business, they say. They can make this claim only by refusing to accept the universal declarations of Scripture (Chapter 3) in conjunction with the exceptions that are found in the broader context of the Bible.

What purpose do generalizations serve? They appear to be self-contradictory. Murder, blasphemy, and many other things were "not permissible" for Paul. How can the Bible say both: "Everything" was permissible for Paul (1 Cor. 6:12) and yet clearly teach that some things were "not permissible" for Paul? How can there be such a flat contradiction in the Bible?

Generalizations are not "contraries." Generalizations reveal the mind-set with which the author is working. They give expression to the perspective from which the matter at hand is to be viewed.

In 1 Cor. 6:12 Paul celebrates the new mind-set of Christian liberty. Paul is no longer a legalist viewing all things as unlawful except what the Law permitted. Paul now has a glorious new perspective, a new freedom in Christ. "Everything is permissible" for Paul, except those things specifically forbidden by God.

A similar purpose is served by the so-called "universalistic" texts (Chapter 3). They reveal the mind-boggling change that has taken place through the work of Christ. Because "one died for all..." we "...regard no one from a worldly point of view" (2 Cor. 5:14–16). We no longer view them in Adam, outside of Christ as children of wrath. We may now view "the world," "all persons," and "everyone" as elect in Christ, as those for whom Christ died, those certain-to-come-to salvation, mindful of the fact that the Bible depicts some who will be finally lost. "For as in Adam all die, so also in Christ all will be made alive" (1 Cor. 15:22).

It is difficult to recognize that our understanding of the Bible's message is colored by the mind-set (the generalization) with which we work. It is even more difficult to change that mind-set. Most of the time we are not even aware of the basic assumption with which we work. Our mind-set will determine *what we see* in the Bible. Remember the goblet on the front cover.

Reacting negatively to what is proposed in this study, the same theologian (See paragraph two, above) wrote: "Salvation is a gift conditional upon response. As in Hebrews 4:2, real good news, but not of benefit until mixed with faith."

This theologian works with the mind-set or assumption that "all persons will be finally lost except those who the Bible declares will be saved." Consequently he draws the following conclusion from Hebrews 4:2: "The good news comes indiscriminately to all persons, those who benefit from it do so *because they believe.*"

Hebrews 4:2 reads: "For we also have had the gospel preached to us, just as they did; but the message they heard was of no value to them, because those who heard did not combine it with faith." Does this verse say that some benefited "*because they believed*?" Or, does it say that some *did not* benefit "because they *refused* to believe?"

Hebrews 4:6 makes it plain that some *did not* benefit "because of their disobedience." The conclusion to be drawn from Hebrews 4:1–7 is that all persons enter into "his rest" except those "whose hearts go astray," and "have not known my ways," they shall not "enter my rest" (Psalm 95:10,11). That is, those who "harden their hearts" when the gospel is "preached to them" (Heb. 4:6,7). The blessing is by sovereign grace, the judgment has to be earned.

The premise we are proposing follows the pattern of God's dealing with the children of men throughout biblical history. God created man good and in a right relationship to himself. "God blessed them" (Gen. 1:28). This blessedness of knowing God and living in fellowship with him was not something conferred upon mankind in response to or merited by obedience. However, this blessedness would no longer be theirs if they willfully walked in disobedience. The blessing was unconditional; the judgment had to be earned.

An unconditional blessing was also promised to the

descendants of Abraham before they were born. "I will establish my covenant as an everlasting covenant between me and you and your descendants after you for the generations to come, to be your God and the God of your descendants after you" (Gen. 17:7). This blessing was "guaranteed" to Abraham and his descendants unless they refused to believe in him or to walk in obedience to him (Rom. 4:16). The blessing was unconditional; the judgment was contingent upon man's action.

The Ten Commandments were not given to the children of Israel so that by keeping them they could merit God's favor. They already were God's adopted children when they received the commandments. "When Israel was a child, I loved him, and out of Egypt I called my son" (Hosea 11:1). They were already the recipients of God's blessing. However, it was also true that if they willfully and finally refused to walk in accordance with God's revealed will they would not experience his blessing.

God's favor at the time of creation, in the covenant with Abraham, and in the affirmation of God's goodness to Israel was not given on the basis of faith, obedience, holiness, or any other good quality in man as a cause or condition for those blessings. In light of this history it is not surprising the good news is that in Christ all persons will be saved except those who the Bible declares will be finally lost. Salvation is by God's grace; condemnation results from the sinner's willful, persistent, evil deeds (Chapter 4).

In conclusion—**We must accept the so-called "universalistic" texts as written.** We can do so as long as we keep in mind the exceptions that are found in the Bible itself. **We may allow only those exceptions that are necessarily**

imposed upon these passages from the broader context of the Scriptures as a whole. (See p. 83)

Discussion Questions:

1. Is Jesus truly human? That is, is he a descendant of Adam?

2. Why is it important that Jesus is an exception to those who were polluted by Adam's sin? How, according to the Bible, was Jesus kept free of Adam's sin?

3. The three schools of thought mentioned in this chapter accept Romans 5:18a as a generalization with an exception. However they insist that Romans 5:18b is a universal with *no* exceptions. Is there any structural or grammatical difference between Romans 5:18a and 18b that makes one a generalization and the other a universal?

4. In what way could this chapter be of help to those who lack assurance of salvation?

5. How does assurance of salvation make one more willing to live the Christian life?

Chapter 6

There Is No "Because" in John 3:16

Through his Spirit and Word the Lord Jesus Christ gathers, defends, and preserves the members of his church. In the obedience of faith, and with the assurance instilled by that faith, believers become fellow-workers in God's kingdom. "The righteous will live by faith" (Rom. 1:17). Faith is a continual and pervasive influence in the Christian life.

The urgency and necessity of faith cannot be overemphasized. The Bible demands that those who hear its message must "repent," "believe," "obey," "come to Christ," "follow him" and so on. But, strange as it may seem, none of these Spirit-directed activities are a prescription or prerequisite for our union with Christ, not even faith.

The Bible neither imposes a condition or prerequisite for sinners to be established in God's grace nor does it indicate how sinful men would be able to fulfill such a condition or requirement. Because these are not found in God's Word, many different ways in which those dead in sin are enabled to believe have been suggested (See Chapter 1).

There is nothing we must do to be saved, that is, there is nothing we can contribute toward our reconciliation with the Creator. Salvation is exclusively God's work. "Therefore, if anyone is in Christ, he is a new creation; the old is passed away, behold, the new has come. All this is from God, who through Christ reconciled us to himself" (2 Cor. 5:17, 18). Martin Luther has correctly observed that we have no more to do with our being born again than we had anything to do with our being born the first time.

That salvation is exclusively God's work completed for us in Christ, and is not dependent on some human act to establish us in the state of grace, is seen in the analogy between Adam and Christ in Romans 5:12–21: "For just as through the disobedience of the one man [Adam] the many were made [Greek—"constituted"] sinners, so also through the obedience of the one man [Jesus Christ] the many will be made [Greek—"constituted"] righteous." No further human act was necessary to make Adam's sin the sin of those he represented, so no further human act is necessary to make the righteousness of Christ the righteousness of those who were represented by him.

Those who will be saved were chosen in Christ Jesus before the foundation of the world. They were redeemed many years ago by the blood of Christ. In accordance with this election and redemption in Christ, the Holy Spirit works the miracle of grace in them. Faith does not bring about this new standing in the grace of God. As important as faith is, this is one thing faith does not do. Faith is the fruit of God's grace already at work in the sinner's heart. "The Lord opened her heart to respond to Paul's message" (Acts 16:14). Faith (the willingness and ability to believe) is some-thing that God graciously gives to those for whom Christ died. "And this is not from yourselves, it is the gift of God—not by works, so that no one can boast" (Eph. 2:8, 9).

Faith is a matter of trusting the good news of God's Word regarding our already established new standing in Christ. This new standing was determined apart from any faith, act, or attitude of ours. It was established by the one "who saved us and called us with a holy calling, not in virtue of our works but in virtue of his own purpose and grace which he gave us in Christ Jesus ages ago" (2 Tim. 1:9). It was long ago that all those who will be saved were objectively saved, as we noted in Chapter 1.

This election does not take place because those who will be saved already were, in some small measure, what God required them to be. They were chosen in order that they may become what God wants them to be: "For he chose us in him before the creation of the world to be holy and blameless in his sight. In love he predestined us to be adopted as his sons through Jesus Christ, in accordance with his pleasure and will—to the praise of his glorious grace, which he has freely given us in the One he loves" (Eph. 1:4–6).

There are times when the above and similar teachings in God's Word appear too complicated for us to bother with. To keep it simple a theologian made the following suggestion: "For a time let us try to forget what God may have done in eternity, and let us see what He has said and done in time through His gracious revelation [the Bible]. Thus we may be able to determine the ground of His discriminations between the finally saved and the finally lost. What does the Bible say? We might cite hundreds of proof-texts, but a few of the outstanding ones will suffice."

This theologian then quotes John 3:16 and other texts that tell us that those who believe in Jesus Christ will be saved. From these passages he, and many others, draw the erroneous conclusion that only those who have a New Testament knowledge of Jesus Christ will be saved. This, they maintain, is the strongest motive for proclaiming the gospel to all persons everywhere and it must be maintained at any and all cost.

We have no right to "forget what God may have done in eternity." Furthermore in John 3:16–18 we again find that there is no condition or prerequisite for salvation. There is, however, a condition or prescription for condemnation (See Chapter 5).

John 3:16 and similar texts are a *description* of the actual situation that pertains to everyone who believes in Jesus Christ. It is a comforting and unshakeable truth that, "Whoever believes in him shall not perish but have eternal life." This declaration does not say, and the Bible *never* says, they "have eternal life" *because* they believe in him. There is no "because" in John 3:16.

There is a "because" in John 3:18: "Whoever believes in him is not condemned, but whoever does not believe stands condemned already *because* he has not believed in the name of God's one and only son." The first part of verse 18, just like John 3:16, is descriptive (it describes the actual situation) and therefore has no "because" in it. The last part of verse 18 *does* have a condition or prescription (a "because") for condemnation. They stand condemned "because" they have not believed. "For the *wages* of sin is death, but the *gift* of God is eternal life in Christ Jesus our Lord" (Rom. 6:23).

Salvation is by grace; condemnation is by works. Precisely in so far as salvation would be conditioned upon the sinner's act of faith, it would not be of grace.

To emphasize the contrast between law and grace, Paul uses the word "faith." We are "justified by faith" and "the promise comes by faith." Why didn't he simply say we are "justified by grace" and "the promise comes by grace"? The answer is that for Jews the law was grace. In his grace (undeserved goodness), God gave the Jews his law, so that by keeping his law they would find acceptance with God. God had not dealt so favorably with any other nation. To say we are "justified by grace" or "the promise comes by grace" would, for the Jews, have the very opposite meaning of what Paul intended.

We do well to use the word "grace" instead of "faith" regarding any blessing that is received by "faith." The Bible never portrays faith as something that merits God's favor. "Therefore, the promise comes by faith, so that it may be by grace and may be guaranteed to all Abraham's offspring" (Romans 4:16). To be saved or "justified by faith" is to be "justified by grace." "There is no difference," everyone who is justified is "justified freely by his grace through the redemption that came by Christ Jesus" (Rom. 3:24).

Some are condemned because they have "not believed in the name of God's one and only Son" (John 3:18b). May we conclude from this fact that all who do not have a New Testament knowledge of Jesus Christ will be finally lost because they have "not believed in the name of God's one and only Son"?

There is a subtle but nevertheless very real hazard in trying "to forget what God may have done in eternity" and to appeal only to the Bible's urgent call to faith. In the very nature of the case only accountable persons, to whom the message of the Bible has been meaningfully communicated, hear the command to believe "in the name of God's one and only Son."

The fact that these persons are required to believe "in the name of God's one and only Son" does not permit us to deduce an essential correlation between such knowledge-able faith and salvation. If such faith were *essential* to salvation, no infant dying in infancy or any mentally challenged person could be saved.

But isn't a personal faith in Jesus Christ necessary for salvation? The answer is an unqualified *yes* for everyone to whom the gospel is presented in a meaningful way. Such a knowledgeable faith is absolutely necessary and unbelief is damnable for them. This is so, not because their knowledge-able faith is a condition for salvation but, because for them to remain indifferent to this revelation of himself that God has given to them would bring God's judgment upon them. Thus they are "justified by faith."

In the very same way *works* justify us. Our "works" merit nothing. But to refuse to do these works is to reject or remain indifferent to God's will for us. Such persistent indifference and rebellion bring the fatal consequence of condemnation (consignment to hell). "You see a person is justified by what he does and not by faith alone" (James 2:24; see also Rom. 1:5; 15:18).

It is not only those who have heard the gospel who can reject God's revelation of himself. It is possible to merit condemnation by rejecting or remaining indifferent to the revelation God gives of himself in nature and conscience (Acts

14:17; Rom. 1:19–25; 2:15–16). God's judgement against them will be just (Rom. 2:5–12).

Although there is nothing we can contribute toward our reconciliation with the Creator, there is much we must do to enjoy that salvation. We must trust God's Word that this reconciliation was accomplished for us. This trust necessarily leads to obedience (Rom. 1:5). We end up necessarily and joyfully doing many things but none of this contributes to bridging the gap between us and God or persuading God to act on our behalf. God "so loved" us before Jesus came into the world "that he gave his Son" (John 3:16).

Might it be better for some persons to remain ignorant of the gospel so they will not reject it? It is true that those who reject the greater truth will receive a greater punishment (Heb. 10:29). But because God cannot deny himself, whatever light he gives by whatever means is the "true light" (John 1:9; Acts 17:23; Rom. 2:14,15, 26). Therefore it is impossible for anyone who has said *yes* to the lesser light of nature and conscience to say *no* to the greater light that beams forth from the gospel. Similarly those who reject the lesser light will reject the greater light (Luke 16:31, Rev. 22:11).

No question of fairness or justice arises out of the revealed cause of salvation or the revealed basis of damnation. On the one hand, God surely has the right to sovereignly and graciously grant his salvation to those whom he will. On the other hand, those who are finally lost have personally, willfully, and persistently chosen to reject or remain indifferent to whatever light has been given to them. They receive the just consequence of their deeds.

However, God's discriminations do not make sense to

us. They are not logical. Those who will be finally saved would have followed the same path as those who are finally lost, if it were not for the sovereign, electing grace of God that gives them the gifts of repentance, faith, and a willingness to walk in God's ways.

How can that be? The answer eludes us, and we may not put God on trial. Believers gratefully recognize that they have no obligation to resolve this perceived problem. One merely traces the lines laid out in God's inspired Word and humbly accepts them.

Discussion Questions:

1. Second Cor. 5:17, 18; Romans 5:12–21; Eph. 2:8,9; 2 Tim. 1:9 and Eph. 1:4–6 are quoted in this chapter. They appear to present complicated teachings. Why would they appear less complicated if we accept the premise, "All persons will be saved except those the Bible declares will be finally lost"?

2. Why is it wrong to "try to forget what God may have done in eternity"?

3. Grace is undeserved favor, freely given. How would the Jews have understood the expression "We are saved by grace"?

4. Is it biblically correct to say "If you believe, God *has saved* you" or "If you believe, God *will save* you"? Are both correct? If both are correct when should we use one and when the other? (Keep in mind objective and subjective salvation, Chapter 1)

5. What significance is there in the fact that there is no "because" in John 3:16 but there is a "because" in John 3:18?

Chapter 7
One Written Word

Although God entrusted his written Word to the church to preserve and proclaim that Word, its message "was preached among the nations, was believed on in the world" (I Tim. 3: 15,16; Col. 1:23b).

> The Bible is a missionary book. This means that in the Bible the Gentile peoples are addressed in a direct and straightforward way. This is the mystery of the Bible, its twofold character. It is a book for the Church, a book that can only be understood by the Church; and it is at the same time a book for the world, a book in which the world is called to believe in Jesus Christ. In the Bible God is wrestling with the world, persuading, reproving, admonishing, beseeching the various people of the world to accept the truth and to be reconciled to God (J. H. Bavinck, The Impact of Christianity on the Non-Christian World, Eerdmans, 1948, p. 139).

The Bible is the one inspired record that reveals the counsel and will of God concerning the redemption of mankind. The promise of the gospel, together with the command to repent and believe, ought to be declared and published to all nations and to all persons promiscuously and without distinction. There is solid theological ground for translating the Bible into as many languages and dialects as possible.

In the Bible the one true God, the only Savior, calls out "Turn to me and be saved, all you ends of the earth; for I am God and there is no other" (Isa. 45:22). The assignment given us is to "make disciples [students] of all nations" and, among other things, teach "them to obey everything I have commanded you" (Matt. 28:20).

"Everything I have commanded you" includes the Sermon on the Mount. In the Sermon on the Mount we are not told, "Live like this and you will become Christian"; rather we are told, "Because you are Christian live like this." All other appeals to ethical conduct in every New Testament epistle are based on this same assumption, namely, that the reader has a new standing with God in Christ.

The reader is not told that his or her ethical conduct will bring him or her to a new standing with God in Christ. What they are required, expected, commanded to do is based on what they are presumed to be in Christ. "Let not sin reign in your mortal bodies" (to do) because "you are not under law but under grace" (presumed to be) (Rom. 6:12, 14). The readers are not to live according to the sinful nature (to do) because "you received the Spirit of sonship" (assumed to be) (Rom. 8:15). They must "put off falsehood and speak truthfully to his neighbor" (to do) because "we are all members of one body" (presumed to be) (Eph. 4:25). "Set your minds on things above" (to do) because "your life is now hidden with Christ in God" (presumed to be) (Col. 3:2, 3) etc.

These appeals to ethical conduct are summed up in the familiar trio of repent, believe, and obey. These calls to new obedience can be called "gospel demands" because they are inseparable from the proclamation of the "good news." These "gospel demands" assume that the one who reads or hears is a new creature in Christ (Chapter 2).

The various people of the world are entreated to accept the truth and to "Be reconciled to God" (2 Cor. 5:18–20). They are not told, "Reconcile yourself to God." The command is passive because, according to verses 18 and 19, there is no human contribution to this reconciliation. "All this is from God, who reconciled us to himself through Christ" (v. 18). "God was reconciling the world to himself in Christ, not counting men's sins against them" (v. 19). "The message of reconciliation" (v. 19) is an announcement, a declaration, or a proclamation of something that God *has done* through Christ. It is not a promise of something God *will do* if and when one believes.

There is nothing sinners must do in order to move God to "not count their sins against them." To "be reconciled to God" sinners must accept (not be indifferent to, or reject) the good news that God has not counted his or her sins against them. On the one hand, this demand can be made only of those who are presumed to have been reconciled to God. On the other hand, this demand is to be made of every person in every nation.

The crucial importance of the fact that the imperative (to do) is based on the indicative (assumed to be) is demonstrated in this analogy: "To say to the slave, who has not been emancipated, 'Do not behave as a slave' is to mock his enslavement. But to say the same to the slave who has been set free is the necessary appeal to put into effect the privileges and rights of his liberation" (Murray, *Romans*, Eerdmans, 1959, p. 227).

The New Testament writers assume that their readers

are no longer slaves of sin. The readers are presumed to have been set free from the power of sin, and they are commanded to put into effect the privileges and rights of those who belong to Christ.

In light of the above truths, we are compelled to choose among the following three possibilities:

Possibility # 1—These demands are imposed only upon a limited number of persons, that is, those assumed to be new creations in Christ. These demands are not placed on the rest of humanity.

This cannot be the answer. God requires these things of everyone who reads the Bible or hears its message. "Let not sin reign in your mortal bodies" is God's will for everyone. No one may live according to his or her sinful nature. Everyone must "put off falsehood and speak truthfully to his neighbor." Everyone confronted with the Word of God is required to "set [their] mind on things above." Gospel demands are not limited to certain individuals: "But now he commands all people everywhere to repent" (Acts 17:30); "We proclaim him, admonishing and teaching everyone with all wisdom, so that we may present everyone perfect in Christ" (Col. 1:28).

Possibility # 2—The same demands and requirements are made of all persons and, for a limited number of persons, these demands are based on their presumed new standing in Christ. The same obedience is required of all other persons on some other basis—perhaps on the basis of their creation in the image of God.

This is not the answer for two reasons. First of all, it

is impossible to demonstrate from the Bible that there is one basis for making these demands of some people and a different basis for some others. Secondly, no other basis is adequate to serve as a basis for these demands.

Possibility # 3–All these demands are addressed to all persons and find their validity and appeal on the same basis.

The premise of Biblical Universalism—that all persons are elect in Christ except those who the Bible expressly declares will be finally lost (See p. 83)—provides the biblical warrant for this third possibility. We may and must assume that everyone we approach with the gospel has a new standing with God in Christ unless or until we have decisive evidence to the contrary.

We must point out that the gospel demands serve a two-fold purpose. They are intended to bring to expression and maturity the new life that is presumed to be in those to whom we bring the gospel (the good news). It is also true that those who finally reject or remain indifferent to "the knowledge of the truth" will receive a more severe judgment (Heb. 10:26, 29). If what is demanded *never* takes place, then, and only then (on the Day of Judgment), will we know that this particular person was one of the exceptions allowed for in our premise.

The Scriptures do not tell us why anyone would want to refuse to have God in their knowledge, or for that matter even how anyone can do so. The Bible speaks of this life-long, self-destructive unbelief and sin as "the secret power of lawlessness" (2 Thess. 2:7). The issue of God's sovereignty and man's responsibility remains unresolved.

There are those who strongly contend that promises, demands and announcements of good news cannot be made to any specific individual or group of persons on the basis of an assumption. They say that person-specific promises and demands can be made only on the basis of a universalization (they would apply to every person without exception) or on the basis of a certainty that this particular person or group has a new standing with God in Christ.

The reality is that it is *only* on the basis of an assumption can we ever say, "Christ died for you" or "Be reconciled to God" to anyone. Universalism and such certainty are never available to us.

Since, on the basis of the Scriptures, we rule out Universalism (Chapter 4), we then need evidence that this particular person or group is necessarily included in God's work of reconciliation before we can say to them "Christ died for you" or "Be reconciled to God."

What kind of certainty would we need? A confession of faith in Christ together with a lifestyle that appears to be consistent with that confession would not be sufficient. This evidence assumes that the person is making a truthful confession. But there are false professors of Christ living apparently godly lives. We cannot judge anyone's heart.

The evidence we would need is some objective, absolute, verifiable proof or certainty that this particular person or group actually is among those who have been reconciled to God through Christ. This kind of proof is never available to us, not even for professing Christians who are closest and dearest to us.

That we are not so limited in saying "Christ died for you," or "Be reconciled to God" is evident from such passages as 1 Corinthians 15:3: "For what I received I passed on to you as of first importance; that Christ died for our sins according to the Scriptures." Paul based this on neither Universalism nor on some absolute irrefutable evidence gained from those to whom he declared it. Paul explained that he passed on to them the message "of reconciliation" (Christ died for our sins) that he had received long before he met the citizens of Corinth (2 Cor. 5:18–21).

What must be exhorted, entreated, even demanded is an appropriate *response* to the good news of what God has already done for the person or persons to whom we present the gospel. The gospel is not a prescription, a suggestion, a proposal that says, "If you repent, believe and obey then Christ will save, redeem, die for you." The gospel is the good news that "Christ has redeemed, saved, died for you, therefore you must repent, believe and live in joyful obedience."

This good news can be declared and published to all nations and to all persons promiscuously and without distinction only on the assumption that all those to whom the gospel comes have been reconciled to God through Christ. That is, the assumption of Biblical Universalism.

Discussion Questions:

1. The "mailing address" on the Bible is "The Church of Jesus Christ." For who else is the message of the Bible intended?

2. Why should we support Bible translation work?

3. What is the dictionary definition of "reconcile"? What instruction or comfort is there is realizing that we do not con-

tribute anything to the work of reconciliation?

4. What the Bible requires of everyone to whom the gospel is presented ("Repent," "Believe," "Be reconciled," etc.) can be done only by those who have been redeemed by the blood of Christ. This lesson presents three possibilities for resolving this apparent problem. What other possible resolution can you think of?

5. To whom do we have biblical warrant (authority, permission) to say, "God loves you so deeply that he gave his Son to die for you so that you may begin a new life in him"?

Chapter 8
Why Preach?

Biblical Universalism allows the possibility that some persons may be saved without having heard the gospel during their lifetime on earth. With this perspective, it is alleged, we lose the strongest motive for proclaiming the gospel, namely, rescuing sinners from eternal death. If sinners can be saved without hearing the gospel, why send out missionaries and why preach?

First, if there is a scriptural basis for Biblical Universalism we must subject our thinking and our actions to it whether, in our opinion, it will stimulate mission enterprise or not. To do otherwise would be to elevate our opinion above the teaching of God's Word.

Furthermore, the above allegation raises some serious questions. Has God determined that no one will be saved except by human proclamation of the gospel? Will the size of our missionary budgets and the quality of our outreach programs determine the number of people in heaven? Will the eternal destiny of some persons depend on whether or not someone made the effort to bring the gospel to them? Even though we know our good works do not save us, are we to believe that those living in non-Christian lands are dependent upon our good works to be saved from eternal death?

Romans 10:14 appears to say yes in response to the above questions. But God's arms are not shortened by the sinful neglect of the Great Commission. Even apart from the gospel mankind "knows God," and "the requirements of the law are written on their hearts"(Rom. 1:21, 2:14–16). Also, if need be, God can cause stones to cry out, donkeys to talk or a star to lead the Magi to Christ. God will accomplish his eternal purposes with or without human means (Psalm 115:3).

In verse 14 Paul challenges the church to get on with its task. "How, then, can they call on the one they have not believed in? And how can they believe in the one of whom they have not heard?" The only revealed means for turning sinners from idols to serve the living God, for enabling sinners to be assured of and to experience the joy of their salvation is the Word preached. Therefore the passage concludes, "How beautiful are the feet of those who bring good news!" (v.15, quoted from Isa. 52:7).

The fact that God has entrusted the task of proclaiming the good news to the church does not mean that God is unable or unwilling to save any among those who would not hear the good news during their earthly life. By sovereign grace, the Holy Spirit can and will create new life in all those chosen to salvation. Jesus will lose none of all those who were given to him (John 6:39).

But the question deserves an answer—Why send Missionaries and preach the Word if all persons who are elect in Christ are certain to come to salvation one way or another? The answer is...

BECAUSE the command of Christ remains the same, "Go

and make disciples of all nations" (Matt. 28:19).

To "make disciples" is to establish a teacher/student relationship. These students must come to know that out of sheer grace, earned (past tense) for them by Christ, not only others, but they too, have *had* their sins forgiven, have *been* made forever right with God and have *been* granted salvation. This knowledge becomes a deep-rooted assurance only by the miraculous work of the Holy Spirit. Therefore, this teaching activity must be continually bathed in the prayers of God's people (Q & A 21 of the Heidelberg Catechism).

These teachers have been given the ministry of reconciliation. They identify themselves with their students in proclaiming that: "God made him who had no sin to be sin for us [teacher and student], so that in him we [teacher and student] might become the righteousness of God" (2 Cor. 5:21). Only on the assumption that both teacher and student have been "reconciled (past tense) to God" can the message of reconciliation be meaningfully communicated to the student.

BECAUSE there is only one gospel (Chapter 7).

No wonder the heavens were radiant with the glory of God the night Jesus was born. The angel announced, "I bring you good news of great joy that will be for all the people. Today in the town of David a Savior has been born to you; he is Christ the Lord" (Luke 2:10).

Jesus was born to the Jews, and therefore the "good news of great joy" was intended for the Jews as God's people. So be it. This takes nothing away from the fact that this same "good news" ought to be declared and published to all nations and to all persons promiscuously and without distinction. With the Holy Spirit upon him, Simeon said, "My eyes have seen your salvation which you have prepared in the sight of all people, a light for revelation to the Gentiles and for glory to your people Israel" (Luke 2:30).

BECAUSE there are those who have been redeemed by Christ among "every tribe and language and people and nation" (Rev. 6:9).

Suppose for a moment that as a missionary you are told of a village of some 150 inhabitants who have never heard the gospel. In some miraculous way, you know that every one of them is an adopted child of God for whom Christ died. Would you avoid this village on the assumption that there is no need to tell them the good news?

When the citizens of Corinth became abusive, Paul was minded to leave without doing further work among them. The Lord told Paul, "I have many people in this city." The result? "So Paul stayed for a year and a half teaching them the word of God" (Acts 18:9–11). Similarly, to view all persons as those for whom Christ died until and unless we have knowledge to the contrary encourages us to teach them the word of God.

BECAUSE every accountable person has a decision to make.

Biblical Universalism recognizes that every sinner has a choice to make. This is not the power of contrary choice. Unbelievers are not in a neutral position from which they can choose good or evil. No one conceived and born in sin has the capacity within himself or herself to choose the good. Those who choose to repent and believe will experience that decision as though they made the decision in their own strength and by their determination of will. However, it is God who "gives them repentance" as he works in them both "to will and to act according to his good pleasure" (Acts 5:31; 11:18; 2 Tim. 2:25; Phil. 2:13).

The decision to reject or remain indifferent to the revelation God gives of himself is made in the sinner's own strength and determination of will. This is so whether this revelation comes through nature (Acts 14:17; Rom 1:19–25), conscience (Rom. 2:15–16), or the proclamation of the gospel (John 5:45–47). Such indifference or rejection sets in motion a hardening process that, if persisted in, ends in eternal death (Chapter 6).

Therefore, with life or death urgency, the church must use the preaching of the Word to persuade all people everywhere to be reconciled to God. Nowhere can sinners see the ugliness of their sin and the astonishing light of God's redeeming love as clearly as in "Jesus Christ and him crucified" (1 Cor. 2:2).

BECAUSE the people of God need to "be thoroughly equipped for every good work" (2 Tim. 3:17).

God wants all of his people to be prepared "for works of service, so that the body of Christ may be built up until we all reach unity in the faith and in the knowledge of the Son and God and become mature, attaining to the whole measure of the fullness of Christ" (Eph. 4:12,13).

Without the "very words of God" (Rom. 3:2) being proclaimed God's will for every aspect of the redeemed sinner's life remains in a significant sense unknown. In the closing portion of Romans 2 Paul speaks of the fact that both those who were circumcised (Jews) and those not circumcised (Gentiles) could either break the law or be praised by God (Rom. 2:25–29). Both covenant people and those outside that covenant fellowship are treated in the same way. No wonder Paul asks, "What advantage, then, is there in being a Jew or what value is there in circumcision?" (Rom. 3:1).

We do no injustice to this question if we ask, "What advantage, then, is there in being a member of the church or what value is there in baptism?" Very significantly, Paul does not answer by saying, "Only among them (those incorporated into the fellowship of the church and receive baptism) is there salvation." Instead, Paul says "Much in every way!" Of first importance, "they have been entrusted with the very words of God" (Rom. 3:2).

The advantage of being a Jew was to be entrusted with the Old Testament as "the very words God." How much greater is the advantage of those who, through the work of missionaries and the preaching of the Word, are entrusted with both the Old and the New Testament as "the very words of God"! Together with this the sign and seal of God's commitment and promise of grace (baptism in place of circumcision) is given to them.

What fellowship, joy, light, comfort, hope, vision, encouragement, peace, nurturing, "teaching, rebuking, correcting and training in righteousness" (2 Tim. 3:16) begin to shape the lives of redeemed sinners by becoming part of the community of believers (the visible church) by way of the work of missionaries! Even if we were given to know that all those living in non-Christian lands were elect in Christ and certain to be saved without hearing the gospel, we would still still have ample reason to bring the good news of what God in Christ has done for them.

Dr. Edward Wm. Fudge accepts the premise of Biblical Universalism and maintains a very significant Internet ministry. In a "gracEmail" (the logo for his ministry) he very graciously and knowledgeably responds to the question we discuss in this chapter.

•　　•　　•　　•　　•

In an earlier "gracEmail," I stated that God will judge all people by the light they had and not by truth they could not know. A missionary in South America asks, "If that is so, am I wasting my time here? Why preach the gospel today? Are you saying that people are saved apart from Jesus Christ?"

Not at all. I am saying that no one will finally be saved except through Jesus Christ and what God accomplished through him. That includes people who lived before Jesus and after Jesus—within Israel and among the nations. That is not to say that all those saved people knew in this life the details of God's work in Christ, although they all did relate to God in the kind of creaturely faith we see in the patriarch Abraham, "the father of the faithful" (Acts 4:11–12; Rom. 2:11–16; Rom. 4:1–16).

Are you wasting your time? No! You are obeying Jesus, fulfilling his Great Commission (Matt. 28:18–20). You are speaking because you believe (2 Cor. 4:13) and are sharing the way of life (Acts 11:18). You are turning people from darkness to light (Col. 1:13–14), introducing people to the living and true God (1 Thess. 1:9–10) and spreading hope of eternal life (Titus 1:1–3). You are giving freedom over fear of death (Heb. 2:14–15), inspiring a living hope (1 Pet. 1:3) and filling people with joy and peace in believing (Rom. 15:13). You are giving assurance of God's mercy that transforms lives (Titus 2:11–15). You are bestowing many, many other blessings through the knowledge of Jesus Christ.

In the process, you are being used by God as an agent in the salvation of those who through your ministry receive the grace of God (2 Cor. 5:18–6:2). The gospel is God's power for saving sinners—in the fullest sense of the word "save" (Rom. 1:16). The kingdom of God brings wholeness and healing of all kinds—spiritual, emotional and physical (Acts 4:10–12). Jesus is the way, the truth and the life (John 14:6). We are privileged to tell people what God has done for them through him, and how God has revealed himself most fully through his only-begotten Son, the divine Word made flesh, Jesus of Nazareth, the Christ. Our success depends on God. His success does not depend on us.

Copyright © 2001 Edward Fudge

· · · · ·

Discussion Questions:

1. How does the distinction between "objective" and "subjective" salvation (Chapter 1) help us "think through" the questions asked in the third paragraph of this chapter?

2. It is said that bad news travels faster than good news. What would account for this?

3. Do Romans 10:9, 10, 13, 14–17 have reference to objective or subjective salvation?

4. What advantage is there in being a member of the church or what value is there in baptism?

5. Do you think Biblical Universalism stimulates or discourages mission and outreach endeavors? Why or why not?

Chapter 9
The Message of Missions

With letters eight inches tall the sign in front of a conservative Calvinist church read:

> ## YOU ARE NOT A NOBODY.
> ## YOU ARE A CHILD OF GOD.

So many questions can be asked about this sign! Was the sign intended *only* for the members of this church? Placed as it was, facing a rather busy street, it apparently was addressed to all who passed by. Is this a greeting that ought to be extended to everyone? Is the sentiment expressed by this sign "The Message of Missions"? One wonders what, if any, biblical/theological consideration went into posting this sign.

For centuries, the church has worked with the assumption that all persons will be finally lost except those who the Bible declares will be saved. This leads us to think that the sentiment expressed by the sign ought to be limited to those who have given some indication that the saving grace of God is already at work in them.

Jesus said, "Do not give dogs what is sacred; do not throw your pearls to pigs" (Matt. 7:6). The apostles were told to "shake the dust off your feet" in protest against those who would not receive them or listen to their words (Matt. 10:14, Acts 13:51). Some individuals, it appears, are unworthy of being told, "You are a child of God."

Furthermore, the need of forgiveness must be felt before anyone can appreciate being told "You are a child of God," implying that their sins are forgiven. Repentance is an essential part of the good news that is to be proclaimed (Mark 1:14,15). These facts seem to require that in outreach ministry we must first tell sinners how great their sin is; secondly, how they can be delivered from their sin; and third, show them how their entire life ought to be an expression of gratitude to God for that deliverance.

Thus, the gospel has become "bad news" accompanied with a good suggestion. The bad news is, "You are a corrupt sinner under the judgment of God's wrath." The good suggestion is, "Believe and you will be saved from your sin."

This view of the message of missions assumes that sinners are not aware of their need for forgiveness. Such is not the case. God has already spoken to all sinners about his wrath. "The wrath of God is being revealed from heaven against all the godlessness and wickedness of men who suppress the truth by their wickedness, since what may be known about God is plain to them, because God has made it plain to them" (Rom. 1:18, 19). "The requirements of the law are written on their hearts, their consciences also bearing witness, and their thoughts now accusing them..." (Rom. 2:15).

Because God's wrath against sin has been made plain to all men, "Many are asking, 'Who can show us any good?'" (Ps. 4:6). Henry David Thoreau was quite right when he said, "The mass of men lead lives of quiet desperation." Why desperation? They are deeply troubled because they know they have provoked the just anger of an awesome power. The extremes to which many have gone in sacrificing their possessions, their bodies and even their own children in order to appease the gods, whom they consider to be against them, testifies to the seriousness with which they view their plight.

In civilized society the wrath of God against the wickedness of men is so effectively suppressed that we have the impression that the unbelievers we meet do not feel the need of forgiveness. It hardly seems that God has made his wrath "plain to them."

Some suppress the truth, and teach their children so, by putting on a good front. They speak of the good they do and that they "try their best." They want to convince others that they are pretty good because deep within they know they are pretty bad. A few try to convince themselves that there is no God out there to whom they are accountable. Others turn to external stimuli of all kinds or to alcohol and other drugs to drown out their conscience. Still others suppress the truth by living in open rebellion against nearly everything their conscience tells them is good.

The apostle Paul appeared to have no qualms of conscience before his conversion. We think he needed to be told, "Saul, you are a blatant sinner on the way to hell, you had better make your life right with God." (The bad news coupled with a good suggestion approach.) But the message that came to him was, "Saul, Saul, why do you persecute me? It is hard for you to kick against the goads" (Acts 26:14). Deep within, Saul was striving against what is good, and it was hard for him to do so. Later he was approached as "Brother Saul" and heard a message of acceptance.

At a deep level sinners are afraid, non-trusting, insecure, and self-defensive. We tend to evaluate these "whitewashed tombs" by their appearance (Matt. 23:27, 28).

What the masses of mankind need to know is that the same holiness that accuses them has provided a full and free forgiveness for their sins. Only then will they dare to admit to themselves, to God, and to others that they are sinners worthy of judgment. John Calvin says, "We mean to show that a man cannot apply himself seriously to repentance without knowing himself to belong to God. But no one is truly persuaded he belongs to God unless he has first recognized God's grace" (Calvin's Institutes, III, iii, 2).

To admit they are grievous sinners worthy of God's judgment is suicidal for unbelievers unless they are first assured that God has removed their sin from them. The instinct of self-preservation does not permit such spiritual immolation. The gospel is the good news for sinners that God *has* redeemed them.

Therefore we should not make God's wrath and judgment against sin the first words in our approach to unbelievers. Jesus was anointed to "preach good news," "proclaim freedom...and recovery of sight," "release to the oppressed," and "proclaim the year of the Lord's favor" (Luke 4:18). Paul says that Christ "came and preached peace to you who were far away [Gentiles, non-Covenant people] and peace to those who were near [Israelites, Covenant people]," because both were reconciled "to God through the cross" (Eph. 2:11–22). "Or do you show contempt for the riches of his kindness, tolerance and patience, not realizing that God's *kindness* leads you toward repentance?" (Rom. 2:4).

When sinners give evidence of remaining indifferent to this good news, or harden themselves against it, God remains gracious as he, through his ambassadors, warns them to flee his wrath that is sure to come upon all who persist in unbelief and sin. This, however, does not mean that we ought to withold the "word of peace" until there is a demonstrated worthiness to receive it.

In Ezekiel's vision there was no evidence of new life among those who would hear his message. He saw dead bones that were "very dry" (Ezekial 37:2). The point of the vision is that Ezekiel was commanded to regard those bones and to deal with them as if they could hear and would live. He was to prophesy to them as though they had the ability to discern and respond to what he demanded of them. "Dry bones, hear the word of the Lord!"

Those who pray that they may elicit a response of faith and joyful obedience from those to whom they proclaim the good news must do so with the assumption that those who hear are elect in Christ. Apart from such a union with Christ there can be no spiritual harvest.

Every congregation and every mission station has had visitors who attend for a while, show interest in joining in fellowship, and then disappear. Later it is reported that while attending they felt like "outsiders." All kinds of initiatives are then suggested and implemented to make certain that everyone feels welcome in "our church." The ads read, "A Friendly Church."

But the problem is much, much, deeper than lack of friendliness or feeling unwelcome. People can feel welcome at the friendly local tavern "where everybody knows your name." Due to the "eyeglasses" the church has worn for centuries we tend to look upon everyone as an outsider until they give evidence of some kinship with us. Although not so intended many of the sermons we hear, the songs we sing and the conversations we have convey this exclusive attitude in little and subtle ways.

To view everyone as child of God for whom Christ died engenders an attitude of oneness far more profound than simply being a friendly church or a friendly person. We must have a positive attitude in outreach ministries. The particular words we may use are not nearly as important as the attitude we have in our approach to unbelievers (1 Cor. 13:1). "Whatever other commandments there may be, are summed up in this one rule: 'Love your neighbor as yourself '" (Rom. 13:9).

With divine authority, we announce the good news that God loves them and has reconciled them to himself in Jesus Christ (Col. 1:19–22). We promise that those who trust God in Christ will experience the joy of salvation (Rom. 10:9–10). We exhort all who will listen to live the redeemed life (Titus 2:11–15). We warn all those who remain indifferent toward or reject this good news that if they so continue there is no hope for them (Heb. 4:6, 7).

The sentiment expressed by the sign referred to above is indeed "The Message of Missions" proclaiming the good news. One would wish, however, that the signboard was big enough and that the human heart and mind were not so crimped by sin, so that those driving by at 45 miles an hour could assimilate the extended message:

> **YOU ARE NOT A NOBODY.**
> **YOU ARE A CHILD OF GOD.**
> **THEREFORE YOU MUST LIVE**
> **LIKE ONE. REPENT, BELIEVE**
> **THE GOSPEL, AND LIVE IN**
> **JOYFUL OBEDIENCE TO HIM.**

Discussion Questions:

1. Although these truths are not an outline for the message of missions, why should Christians know how great their sin is, how they are delivered from their sin, and how to express their gratitude to God for this deliverance?

2. Why is it that an unbeliever "cannot apply himself seriously to repentance without knowing himself to belong to God"?

3. In what circumstance should unbelievers be warned "to flee the wrath of God"?

4. Why is it more important to have church members view all persons as children of God than to express this sentiment by a sign in front of the church? We know how to change a sign, but how can we change our views?

5. Should we ever speak of "outsiders" visiting "our church"? What do we mean by referring to some persons as "outsiders"? And is it really "our church"?

Chapter 10
Thinking Further

In this last chapter we will consider three topics that come to mind when thinking about the premise of Biblical Universalism.

FEW or MANY. Neither the traditional premise nor the perspective we propose (See Introduction) speaks directly to the question of whether few or many will be saved. Premise "A" seems to imply that many (perhaps most) will be finally lost. Premise "B" appears to say that many (perhaps most) will be saved.

Nothing is gained by speculating about "few" or "many." It may be useful, however, to consider why the impression that proportionally few will be saved is rather common. The first reason is the fact that ever since the fourth century most theologians have worked with the premise, "All persons will be finally lost except those who the Bible declares will be saved" (Chapter 1).

Another reason is that scarcity increases the value of most things. Antique collectors are well aware of this. At one time salt was so scarce it was used as money. The chemical composition of salt has not changed, but it is so plentiful it can no longer be so used. If diamonds were as plentiful as gravel, we might pay someone to haul them away from our property. Because salvation is so extremely valuable, we are biased toward thinking it must be scarce.

Salvation is not scarce: "Where sin increased, grace increased all the more" (Rom. 5:20). Its price is right: "Come, buy wine and milk without money and without cost" (Isa. 55:1). The assurance is given: "For everyone who asks receives, and he who seeks finds, and to him who knocks it will be opened" (Matt. 7:8). The command is: "Go out to the roads and country lanes and make them come in, so that my house will be full" (Luke 14:23). The invitation we hear is "The Spirit and the bride say, 'Come!' and let him who hears say, 'Come!' Whoever is thirsty, let him come; and whoever wishes, let him take the free gift of the water of life" (Rev. 22:17).

To portray the great value of salvation the kingdom parables picture entrance into the kingdom of heaven as something that is hard to find, rare and difficult to attain. It is depicted as a treasure hidden in a field and pearl of great value (Matthew 13:44, 45). Neither of these two parables, however, lead to the conclusion that few persons will be saved.

"But small is the gate and narrow the road that leads to life, and only a few find it" (Matt. 7:14). Does this parable of the two ways mean that the way is hard to find because the gate is small, that entering the kingdom is difficult because the road is narrow, and that rarely does anyone enter because it says, "few find it"?

The Kingdom is not hard to find; everyone "who seeks" finds it. It is not difficult to attain because to all who knock "the door is opened." It is not limited to a few because "everyone who asks, receives" it (Matthew 7:7, 8). The "small gate," "narrow road," and "few" finding convey the same thought as the "hidden treasure," and the "pearl of great value."

These figures of speech are not calculations regarding the number of persons who will be saved. They are intended teach us to covet salvation as a rare discovery, an invaluable treasure; to be willing to forsake all other interests in order to attain it. An attitude of thoughtlessly drifting along with the crowd through a wide gate is a sure sign that one is not on the road that leads to glory.

The observation has been correctly made that there is no more reason to conclude from the parable of the two ways that few will be saved than there is to conclude from the parable of the ten virgins (Matt. 25:1–13) that precisely as many will be saved as will be finally lost.

We must also consider Matthew 22:14: "For many are invited, but few are chosen." This is a conclusion to the series of parables (Matt. 21:33–22:13) that precede it, as the word "for" indicates. These parables include those of the tenants, the cornerstone, and the wedding banquet.

In these parables Jesus is speaking of the leaders of Israel (Matt. 21:45) as representing "his own." The theme of each of these parables is, "He came to that which was his own, but his own did not receive him" (John 1:11). The religious leaders and most of God's covenant people did not respond favorably to Jesus' earthly ministry.

This evil was overruled for good, as we see in the ministry of Paul and Barnabas: "We had to speak the word of

God to you first. Since you reject it and do not consider your-selves worthy of eternal life, we now turn to the Gentiles" (Acts 13:46, 47). "For many are invited, but few are chosen" refers to the fact that few of his countrymen responded to Jesus' invitation and therefore many from among the Gentiles were invited and came.

ASSURANCE OF SALVATION. We can have full assur-ance of salvation only when we come to know that salvation is entirely God's work. To base assurance of salvation on anything other than, or in addition to, God's completed work in Christ subjects the believer to perpetual uncertainty.

Our faith or even our decision to believe does not save us. Our faith, as well as such a decision, is a fruit of our union with Christ. By the time a person is so changed that he is willing to accept God's grace he is no longer the old man, the natural man, who regards the gospel as foolishness. Such a person already has a new heart that causes him or her to recognize the "good news" as wisdom that comes from God.

The personal act of faith, in so far as it is a human act, is still tainted with sin. Even our best works are as "a pollut-ed garment." Nothing that is tainted with sin can be *essen-tial* to our salvation. As we noted in Chapter 6, there is no "because" in John 3:16. "It [salvation] does not, therefore, depend on man's desire or effort, but on God's mercy" (Rom. 9:16).

How grateful every Christian should be that their sal-vation does not depend on his or her faith. There are many sincere Christians who are neither indifferent toward nor do they reject the promises and claims of Christ in the gospel.

Nevertheless, they find it difficult to come to the assurance of salvation. Because they have been taught that the gospel is a conditional promise they are plagued by doubts: "Do I love him enough?" "Is my faith strong enough?" "Have I truly repented?" "Am I fully committed to Christ?" "Will I remain faithful to the end?" Trusted friends hear them say, "If you only knew how sinful I am!"

Conditional salvation leads to pride in those who think they have fulfilled the required conditions. Those who correctly sense that they do not have the power within themselves to meet such conditions feel that there is no "good news" for them.

Although not so intended, it is cruel to say to those who have difficulty coming to assurance of salvation, "Well, you believe, don't you?" It is the person's faith, or the strength of that faith, they are questioning. It is no comfort to the person whatsoever to tell them that their salvation depends on their faith!

The response of Biblical Universalism to all who sincerely inquire about their lack of assurance of salvation is this: "The gospel is meant for you unless you are indifferent toward it or willfully reject it." They may be assured that no sin or weakness (including the weakness of their faith) that remains in them against their will can hinder them from being received of God in grace and being worthy partakers of the cup of salvation.

THE NEED FOR SELF-ESTEEM. Theological insights are not useful to God. If they do not help us give greater praise to God and to live more joyfully in his presence we need have little to do with them.

Among other things, Biblical Universalism provides us with a proper sense of self-esteem. This need for recognition finds its roots in the fact that we have been created in the likeness of God, who does all things for his own glory.

Corrupted self-esteem is sinful pride. One would be hard pressed to know of any evil that has been more pervasive and done more harm than sinful pride. Self-esteem has a great potential for good and therefore, when distorted by sin, it has a great potential for evil.

Proper self-esteem is not to be rejected. It must be restored to its God-given role by the renewing power of the Holy Spirit according to the following biblical guidelines:

1) Proper self-esteem is a biblically defined view of oneself as a child of God—fully that and never anything more than that.

2) It is only by a vital redemptive relationship to Jesus Christ that a person can have positive self-esteem.

3) Such a self-image is essential to everyone's spiritual and psychological wellbeing.

4) Both within the church and in evangelistic outreach the gospel must be communicated so as to engender a positive self-image in those who hear it.

The biblical witness to such a view of self-esteem is clear: "How great is the love the Father has lavished on us, that we should be called children of God! And that is what we are!" (1 John 3:1). God wants his followers to respect themselves as equal children of God and to treat all other human beings with the same respect.

Due to mankind's sin in Adam (original sin), everyone by nature has a negative self-image. This negative view of oneself is not the essence of sin, but it is a by-product of sin. It manifests itself in many different ways, such as: pride, anxiety, fear, anger, hopelessness, hate, and mean rebellion.

Biblical Universalism provides the only basis we need for viewing ourselves and every person we meet as a child of God for whom Christ died, unless we have final and decisive evidence to the contrary. As long as we remain in this life, we will not have such knowledge to the contrary regarding any person or group of persons. A ministry of affirmation and acceptance, structured on this biblically warranted assumption, engenders a positive self-image in those who proclaim and in those who hear it.

DISCUSSION QUESTIONS:

1. Why do you think Jesus avoided the question, "Lord, are only a few people going to be saved?" (Luke 13:23).

2. What other things, besides salvation, are not scarce but nevertheless are very valuable?

3. "Let go and let God" is presented as a popularized way of coming to an assurance of salvation. What do you think of this advice? Why is this advice found in Luke 18:9–14?

4. Do you think the four guidelines for establishing a good self-image are biblical?

5. Many Christians frown upon a gospel of proper self-esteem. In light of 1 John 3:1 is this an acceptable Christian attitude? Why or why not?

If the perspective we considered in this study has validity, it will take the Christian community many years to fill in and work out all the details of what is presented. Our hope is that the reader will carefully examine what has been presented in the light of the written Word of God. In doing so, may each one find encouragement and joy in a God-glorifying way of under-standing the good news of salvation.

Textual Index

BIBLICAL UNIVERSALISM is the teaching that all persons are elect in Christ except those who the Bible expressly declares will be finally lost, namely, those who ultimately reject or remain indifferent to whatever revelation God has given of himself to them whether in nature/conscience or in gospel presentation.

Biblical Universalism is based upon three biblical facts:

1) The so-called "universalistic" texts speak of a certain-to-be-realized salvation as Calvinists have consistently maintained, and they do so in terms of all persons as Arminians have always affirmed (Chapter 3).

2) All persons, except Jesus Christ, are liable for and polluted by the imputed sin of Adam (original sin). However, the Scriptures do not teach or imply that anyone is consigned to eternal damnation solely on the basis of their sin in Adam *apart from* actual, willful, and persistent sin on the part of the person so consigned (Chapter 4).

3) We must accept the so-called "universalistic" texts as written. We may allow only those exceptions that are necessarily imposed upon these passages from the broader context of the Scriptures as a whole (Chapter 5).

This study is based on the following two books by Neal Punt:

Unconditional Good News, Toward an Understanding of Biblical Universalism, Wm. B. Eerdmans Publishing Co., 1980 ISBN 0-8028-1835-8 [Out of Print]

What's Good About The Good News? The Plan of Salvation in a New Light, Northland Books, 1989 ISBN 0-945315-07-4 [Available at Northland Books, Box 63, Allendale MI, 49401, Amazon.com, or Barnes and Noble]

Helpful Hint for Group Leaders

When Biblical Universalism is first introduced there will be many questions raised. Most of these will be addressed in a future chapter. Leaders can be prepared by reading all the chapters before beginning a class.

Contact the author at:
whenindoubt@novagate.com

Visit the Biblical Universalism website at:
www.novagate.com/~whenindoubt

So Also In Christ